Also by Susana Gardner

to stand to sea (The Tangent Press, 2006)
SCRAWL Or,- (from the markings of) the small her(o) (Dusie, 2006)
da Scarabocchio o, (dalle valutazioni del) piccolo erosu(o) (HGH, 2008)
[lapsed insel weary] (The Tangent Press, 2008)
EBB Port or, Sonnets from Her Port (Dusie, 2007)
Herso (The University of Theory and Memorabilia Press, 2009)
Hyper-Phantasie Constructs (Dusie, 2010)

Herso

AN
HEIR
INSHIP
WAVES

Susana Gardner

www.blackradishbooks.org

The author would like to gratefully thank the editors of the following publications, where versions or variations of poems from this book have appeared: Eiríkur Örn Norðdahl (NTAMO, Iceland); Boris Jardine, Lydia Wilson and Emily Critchley (Cambridge Literary Review, England); Bruce Covey (Coconut, USA); Harry Godwin (Cleaves Journal, UK); John Clark (In their Own Words, UK); Frances Kruk, Redell Olsen (How2, UK); Rebecca Wolff, Catherine Wagner (Fence Books, USA); Marco Giovenale (HGH/:GAMMM, Italy); Dana Teen Lomax (Kindergarde, USA); John Tranter, Pam Brown (Jacket, UK, AUS); Jill Stengel (mem, USA); James Davies, Tom Jenks and Scott Thurston (The Other Room Anthology, England); Nicole Mauro (University of Theory and Memorabilia Press, USA), and the collective publishing endeavours of the Dusie Kollektiv, Black Radish Books and Delirious Hem.

Cover and book design by Susana Gardner and Black Radish Books.
Cover image: *Come Wander with Me*, Margaux Kent

*for Stella
and for Andrea and Sarah,
my sisters*

First Printing, 2011 in the United States of America.

ISBN: 978-0-9825731-4-3
LCCN: 2010915809

Black Radish Books, USA

CONTENTS

Froward

'It's the sea that brought me, little heart of mine...Stop wave-beat, stop heart-beat.'

Isak Dinesen, *Tempests*

Our thus paired open country.
   Sea cupped hours at tea tide.
   Wake. garnered. dream-white.

Noting but Idea… time steeped
No things pictured mottled or…
Garnet waves and
   Apparitions of she,
   her here.

Say, silhouetted she there again,
at dusk, elliptically held in the frame,
triangular beauty, her kid-gloves knotting
not one thing—whereby purplish-blue
light-held shadows alight tidings of…
   Say starlings,-
   Say sparrows,-

Canvas staid. Open. Said. Staid. Fast. Canvas repeat.
Bundle curled in her lap. But,- our manied years,
once singular, strayed I, became she — attempting
to call or recall the ego herein, attempting to
finish herself off.
   Say Time's keeper.
   Say Time keeps her.
   Say Time was what had

Ever kept her. Summation, redux…
   Always the Seanow —Seaheld.
   Wary. Mild dew-eyed,
   Starry shore-width child.

Her timeless sea-cups colluded and collided thus.
Consequently crashing in and in Untamable as
changeling*stark*winged tender — nothings first conversing.
Away from the sea now, *as we now,* as we look toward her…
   Ruby large,- enow — her
   Gaze, the sea there — Herso
   In sea-bald in sea-feld fields,
   She-sped patterned momentures —

thee thee thee thee thee thee thee thee thee thee thee thee thee
thee thee thee thee thee thee thee thee thee thee thee thee thee
thee thee thee thee thee thee thee thee thee thee thee thee thee
thee thee thee thee thee thee thee thee thee thee thee thee thee
thee thee thee thee thee thee thee thee thee thee thee thee thee
thee thee thee thee thee thee thee thee thee thee thee thee thee
thee thee thee thee thee thee thee thee thee thee thee thee thee
thee thee thee thee thee thee thee thee thee thee thee thee thee
thee thee thee thee thee thee thee thee thee thee thee thee thee
thee thee thee thee thee thee thee thee thee thee thee thee thee
thee thee thee thee thee thee thee thee thee thee thee thee thee
thee thee thee thee thee thee thee thee thee thee thee thee thee
thee thee thee thee thee thee thee thee thee thee thee thee thee
thee thee thee thee thee thee thee thee thee thee thee thee thee
thee thee thee thee thee thee thee thee thee thee thee thee thee
thee thee thee thee thee thee thee thee thee thee thee thee thee
thee thee thee thee thee thee thee thee thee thee thee thee thee
thee thee thee thee thee thee thee thee thee thee thee thee thee
thee thee thee thee thee thee thee thee thee thee thee thee thee
thee thee thee thee thee thee thee thee thee thee thee thee thee
thee thee thee thee thee thee thee thee thee thee thee thee thee
thee thee thee thee thee thee thee thee thee thee thee thee thee
thee thee thee thee thee thee thee thee thee thee thee thee thee
thee thee thee thee thee thee thee thee thee thee thee thee thee
thee thee thee thee thee thee thee thee thee thee thee thee thee
thee thee thee thee thee thee thee thee thee thee thee thee thee
thee thee thee thee thee thee thee thee thee thee thee thee thee
thee thee thee thee thee thee thee thee thee thee thee thee thee
thee thee thee thee thee thee thee thee thee thee thee thee thee
thee thee thee thee thee thee thee thee thee thee thee thee thee

Herso

it is always the same coastline –
with its unsteady
grayed forecast – coastline
carried   and   kept
changeless   as the
sea is   forward and
same – thus
descending   as the
sea must seemingly descend
as in its coastal carriage –
each wave wearily catching and
crashing into the next –
a hatching – a harmony or honing
(if you will) of this we   this coast
this I – long abandoned – a nest
or home ever as even as it is just –
only ever built in anticipation of
its eventual   unraveling of each
moment in its remaking – a simple moment
a cunning moment   thus defined
as the road is steep   this road is blind
and never ending of   sea same
sea   sane   sea erratic

see her home as heedful, or,-
toward her intention of desire
or,-   as an inevitable creational
turning   which comes when
straw and feather   when hair
leaves   bits   of dirt-moss and
plastic intertwine toward her
state of/or   here : matted dry
(and so haphazard)   together :
this she she never knew or was
but founded anew – toward the
page   (the sea-lit heart) rises
receding and so forward slowly
ever-still   as language must and
so forth

what is ever yet at hand,- ever yet
held – and thus unevenly promenad-
ing, say the sea, say another precious
element say gray in its many   varied
casts   as the sea was only ever un-
toward her   and unyielding   as long
seemingly broken – a preternatural
piece-work of every moment nearly
shattered and abandoned – and every
other quickly slapped back together –
only to be withdrawn again,- or
simply left in its relentless lapsing
always left   for the past for the
future of – the present pretty and that
which surrounded it – again,-

summoned like prayer in a desperate
hour – the sea was true and there –
a l o n e – enveloping and about all
pain in the hours before she came – in
its steady bent beat and refrain – with
urgency – so toward– so untold – not
which came but that which came as
now as real and new – what   hard fast
natural marks did each   breath
touch – as so to push or breathe in
the way it should – each previous breath
– intense and over-lapping – stalking its
new predecessor – endless hours – an
entire day – what was once unwanted
so wavering   was now so – this new I,
small hero.

an infantine picture – made actual – in
its clarification of what simply is,- and
so already cast preordained before it
could be painted or designed – such
as a postcard life might be – notes and
marginalia   as scrawled hedge work
of tomorrow – knew – what   so ripe
forthcoming – what consumes – what
still was I and I of self and I ever self-
same dull referencing point now became
new as every previous solipsism curt-
sied again and again toward its
impending erasure, *a d i e u* –

       a d i e u –

f a r e w e l l –
said this new stranger – as she rewrote
all others (alongside each previous
self) in her perfect silence in which she
came alongside the others – their small
cries (of birds) – really like the cry
of birds and stark morning light – she
bade them goodbye – only then could
I understand this (her) new need to
come negating any previous query – as
to why – when she first uttered,-

'eh

eh

eh' –

'eh eh eh' – tiny bird – provok-
ing – *rara avis* – established the need
to memorize this moment – her face
– presented itself like no other – not to
– but through – me – weary exigencies
– like no other in the first hours,- and
the sea so still then when we were on
but the edge of earth but there as still it
might have been quite present and true
in its presiding – among far distant
cool gray blue waves lapping so blue-
gray slate and undaunted,- this absent
coast of my birth – so so – as though
it were dared by she who was now so
close so real and perfectly bundled her
package and design which could have
never been pre-thought or imagined
– 'eh eh eh' and now   nestled under
bird-light – latched
under-wing –

perhaps there is only gray in what we
must name experience – in what we
site as meaning or wayward curiology –
yet before this time I only saw   black
as black or white as white   though
gray might certainly and often overtake
me – much more often was caught on
the edge of what is so easily nicked –
never felt or desired as it should have
been (as what I see now) this possibility
of self this I (I suppose) seems more
central more relevant as it does more
searchingly loyal and narrow in its
slant toward the creeping light – the
shadows after – and all new exploration
– every previous draft – mere lapsed
feathery happenstance

as   what first
seemed
so clear
so raw
as what
had always
took me by the pants
to this present place of occupation
(waxed seeming surprise)
a place to which I
must now hold as keeper –
to think, to never know
e v e n,   (yes,- even) seems
ludicrous – as to
not know
dawn –
ever – to
write it here
as – but what
before it was
so breathtakingly
clear – so stunning and
seductive

of what is moderate   and middling was
and why I had never found   further
meaning   as I had never known that
which could be more than speculation
as what is more spectacular than I had
ever hoped or known by the very
moment in its occurrence
in its reassurance   and – the sea – the
sea still   – the sea sane –   in its   dis-
crete and volatile way – is always the
sea – no matter – how long or far I
must depart from it – it is always there
and present – but something which only
she could access and reify

which held itself still for   so many
years – once before me – as wayward
and taunting – this reflection of others –
and still,   so new   so yet unturned – in
way of her arrival as truth   so truced
this new beginning her voice resonating
as the bells   of each hour   might –
new language hanging upon the edge of
the air in its own way – say presence
say   now   say yet   say   tomorrow

Herso

An HeirShip
Of Mostly
Girthish Sighs
with Irrational
Lithographies

The inhibitance of the body

                      thee
      thee
                                  thee
               thee

inhibitance – structural wants: inhabitance

    prescient laker   currency   tattered

wherewithal   whatnot   tended

      missiles   lacker missives
      shedust   she wantless
      shemoment   motto so feels less

once dreamt: a field

wherewithall   *herso*   isolate

waldheim

she ap*parent*less   *sta*rts

once spent

wie so

heimweh

wood abandon

herso n *is ships*

she fastidious
      openthroated
sherepeat
      leaf open
repents
      starsick
she waves
      half-averse

dame bequested
      latchkey heirship
moss entangled
      burgeon shoot
dame steady ruby
      throated proliferant
waves she
      begotten

only half-imagined
            ontologic
quarter-noted side-steps

(steeped half-breaths)

herso stutterances

one one one

half uttered changeling

half hesitant fee-child

alone in the world heralding

one one one
(on repeat)

one one one
(shefalters remembrance)

one one one
only in (in*her*itance)

one one one
(shestar, she starling, she haltingly so)

one one one
(small *her*o gathering)

one one one
(herso repeat, look up)

(Her)Unisons*Hers*Unisons

SUNRushNosier*ShushShushSirensSiren*Sunriseshone*Sunrise*thine
SunriseHonesInuresInsuresHonsSinesOnrushSinsHornsNon
UsersHisinSunNeurons*HisHisHis*sEhRosinsNus*Eh*RosinsSun*Eh*
RuinsSons*Eh*SirsNounsHeInnsSoursHeIronsSunsHeRosinSuns*Eh*

HeRosinsSun
He*RuinSous*
HeNounsSurs
HeSirsNouns
Shiner*NosUs*
ShinerSonUs
S*hiner*Nus*oS*
Shin*er*SunS*o*
S*hiner*UN*S*os
ShrineNosUs
S*hrine*Son*Us*
S*hrine*Nu*s*So
ShrineSunSo
S*h*rine Nu Sos
S*h*rines*NoUs*
S*h*rine*sShiner*OUR*hrs*

Shores

Shores Shores I shores in Shores Shores I shores
in Shores Inn Shores Is Shores Shores I shores in
Shores Inn Shores Is Shores Shores I shores in
Shores Inn Shores Is Shores Shores I shores in
Shores Inn Shores Is Shores Inn Shores Is Shores
Shores I shores in Shores Inn Shores Is Shore in
Horses I Horses I Horses In Sun Horses Inn Us
Horses Sin Horses Ins Hearses Her Seas Horses Is
Hers is *Herso* is Shore

Sunshines Or,-

An Inshore Farm
Our Heroine's Suns
And so.
Her Her Her.
Her(o)ine.
Das
inn inn
in a Swift,
sharp, polyvocalic
she she in sweeps.

by sea on...

by the sea on...
nested sea on.
nets her sea on...
nests the sea on...
by sea on...
nested sea on...
nets her sea on...
by the sea on...
by the sea on...
nested sea on.
nets her sea on...
nests the sea on...
nested sea on.
nets her sea on...

AN HEIRSHIP
OF MOSTLY GIRTHISH SIGHS
Or,- Sheerer Lightships of Girlish Rigors

Peregrines Telephonies A Prehensile High Shirr star
Replenishes Rigors Sir,-Gosh Hiss Slight Heresies with
Light Plot Shorn Is Sirs Hilted Prisons Lightships His
Nor High Shorn Pistils Hints Hops Hints PoshThins
Hops A Sheerer Rigorous Holding Hips Shirts Leerier
Highs Ships Norths Elegies Ships Shirr A Peregrine
Shh Shh Iris Slot Energies *Shh Shh* List Prior A Genteel
Shh Shirr Hops Iris A Genteel *Shh Shh* Sprightlinesses
Literarinesses Selenographers Solitarinesses Selenog-
raphies Priestlinesses Lithographies Healthinesses
Heartlessness Surly Selenographer Personages with
Plaudits Stenographies Stenographers Elephantiasis
Ghastly Tiny Teenaged Wonting Transgressors An-
gioplasties Sprightliness Ghostlinesses Girlishnesses
Elephantiases Complicated Relationships Harken-
ing Shapelinesses and Garish Wasted Lithographers
Hoarsenesses Personalties Sheepishness Preregisters
Politenesses Telegraphers Peregrinates Lithospheres
Prehistories Respiration Peasantries Tirelessness
Sisterlinesses Alterions Priestliness Telegraphies
Greasepaints Heartlessnesses Tastinesses Generosities
Paltrinesses Repossessing Proletarians Relationship
Generalships Lightnesses Interlopers Peered Generosities
Hastiness Earthinesses Sprightlinesses Retrogresses
Parishioners Transgressor TransgressesPitilessness
Grislinesses Lithographer Separateness Solitariness
Literariness Garishnesses Greasinesses Reassertions
Hopelessness Stenographer Enterprises Straplesses
Shapeliness Artlessness Rightnesses Parenthesis
Isinglass Vestiges Stale Harshnesses Haptic Hapless
Nephritises Lithosphere Relegations Stainlesses Peas-
antries Aspirations Northerlies Restrainers Regres-
sions Salesperson Interlopers Linearities Hastiness-
es Repertoires Parentheses Ghostliness Seigniorial
Sparenesses Telegrapher Genialities Agelessness Re-
plenishes Singletrees Repertories Sprightlier Parish-
ioner Reparations Trespassers Passionless Respira-
tion Sophistries Telephonies Pastinesses Sharpnesses
Shortnesses PrearrangesPageantries Earlinesses
Saltinesse Hairinesses Hairsprings Sorrinesses
Greasepaint Peregrinated Reassertions Forever Reas-
serting Airless Generalists and Girlish Petaled Tipsi-

nesses Peristalsis Peristalses Rotisseries Seniorities
Iratenesses AlertnessesSoapinesses Shoestrings Pro-
letarian Patronesses Separations Healthiness Phi-
listines Telephoners Preregister Intersperse Reas-
sessing Itineraries Ghastliness Signatries Irrigations
Hoarinesses Splashiness Espaliering Trespassing
Dowagers Respirators Largenesses Anesthesias Lithe-
nesses Pithinesses Lightnesses RearrestingLegionar-
ies Greatnesses Perihelions Priestesses Repressions
Without Endings Plagiarists

HEIRSHIPS

Rotary Orphanages Rehearsing
Our blatant rationales Rehearings Rehearsary Trespasses or Telegraphing Whorsaries Sheath Plasterings Outer Sharpies Serigraphing Thrash Ceiling Policings Perkiness and Odd Tailoring Transships Rehearsals Rephrasing Repression Airinesses Interloping Shoestring Earthiness Prioresses Retrogressing Parentages Which Transpires Politeness Which Transpires Horsehair Respirator--Asperities Our Polarities Heathenish Oh, Our Peregrine Senilities

Shorelines Garnishing Sparseness
Senatorial Plagiaries Oh,- Garnishing Reparatory Aspirators ancient Grisliness HER Holinesses and Naturlich Salinities HER Easterlilies Inhaling Regression HER Easinesses Greasiness Apostasies Hilarities Ripenesses Personages Parsonages Restraining *OR- **ROSY SLING-SHOT OPTIMISM**

Plagarist Heartiness in Portlines
Wager Echoes Threading Dive Spirited Banshees Pressure of Preserving Autonomous Earbleeding Visionary Desolation Oh, Interloping Generators Sans Registries Aerialists Sparsities feddered Latent Sirs,-

Persisting Histrionic Gory Lightships
Her Once pleasanter Transpolar ShoesString Happinesses Colliding Prehensile Perihelion Transgressing Porringers Hostessing Separation Repression Borderline Personalities Presenting Realnesses Her Spiritless Assertations Her Gory Lightship Psalteries Repeating Repenting-- Oh, Inheritors Prae-

torian Hers Pressing Resistless Prosthesis Prosthe-
ses Springiest Priestlier Latenesses Raptnesses Hol-
stering Glossiness Lethargies Antisepses Giantesses
Resharpens Glossaries of indexed Sleepiness Time
Progresses Reserpines Preheating Sorenesses Her
Astonished Perdition Oh, Peritoneal Prissiness Horse-
tailing Any Pseudo Sportiness Sheltering Hailstones
Heptagonal Whatifs Reptilians Wives Consorting Tear-
gas Serenities Over Aeroplanes Glassy Priorities, Oh
Wicked Hasheeshes

Trespassers of Singletree PassionateVictuals

Relegators of
All Eastern Artsiness My False Harlotries Essential
Sightseers of Philistine Enterprise Oh, Slithering
Paltriness– Highnesses Rearranges Solitaries Report-
ing Nasalities Generalist Plasterers Hidden in Farm-
Holes Replete with Daily Songstresses of Anesthesia
Stepback Harken olden Nostalgias Passengered Slath-
ering Rotisserie Separators Aspirating Orangeries
Possessing Presorting Rosary Phantasies Registrars
Repertoire of Starlight Please Telephone Her Paleness-
es Her Transpositioning Bifurcated Dogma During
Preseasons Half-time Oh Rash and Irrational Parathi-
on Oilinesses Blotting Paper Phalangers Esophageal
Politesses Boistering Solitaires Hairsprings

Antiheroes

Telephoning Seaward Lonely
Separatists- Must Interpose Economies Aspersions
Lithographing Originates Lighteners Serrations
Stranglers Aspiration Garish Sergeants Tattling
Economists Reorienting Dotstartups... Rehearing
Listserv Sheernesses False Prophets Be Done – Our
Aerial Largesses Have Arrived– Lightship Pathogens
Originals Thrashing Shapelier Slingshot Strapless
Atrophies Represses Greatness Strangler Grisliest
Strangers Topiaries Threshers Gatherers Strainers
Resonates Reasserts Separator Honesties Personals
Resisting Religions Peasants Parsonage Gasolenes
Slangiest Shoestring Offering Questionable Histori-
ans

TailspinsFaltering

Lengthier Tran-
spire Portieres Threshing Garroters Reinserts Gelati-
nous Sirs--Sharpened Transship Repletion Herniators

Parentages Assignors Reportages Hairlines Plasterers Reheating Progenies Assertion Rehearses Plethoras Relations Perihelia Sheetings Tarragons Ingresses Organists Grassiest Sartorial Nostalgia Stressed Hastiness Elongates Parathion Reprisals Ghastlier Steerages I Sing Lasses Sheathing Anopheles I sing Intaglios Iraten Stinging Preschoolers Seaing Hosieries Rightness Regatherers Pointed Lighthouse Keepers of Island Peace Splintering Irrigates Peignoirs Roastings Interpose Realities Halitosis Retailing Seaplanes Interiors Heptagons Signposts

Starlings Airplanes Ligations Estrogen Nations Registering Gendered Partnerships of Estranged Leprosies Lingerers Responders Essential Terniary Lightships Espresso Shooting Rationals Toward Thespian Slippage Respiring Porringer Staleness Sightless Seigniors Seashores Heightens Paginated Personages Heliports Reporters Sprinters Prissy Sheen of Shapeless Shirrings Springier Shanghais Patronesses Resilient Signalers Ghostlier Reentries Epithelia Triangles Alertness Reifying Our Long-True Grapeshot Heroes

Sirens Anthered Lineage Egrets and Asters and Asters O Starling! Astras and Estering Pierships Ported Nests Strop Heals Tenor Poets Loiterers Arsonists Tolerators of the Untolerable and Prisoner Partisans or Palatine Oriental Hostelers Nihilists Idealist Seahorse Assigners Readers Plagarist Listenhers

Her Days Heritages

Noiseless

Graphites
Spinsters
Ghostlest

Heartless
Senseless
Inhalators
Regresses
Shortness
SeaShows

Relenting

Restraints

OOOOOO OUR
GRANARIES
ARE IGNITING
Barbie Heiresses
Plenaries Phalanger
Fakewinds Aspi-
rates Rehearsals
Telegraphs Pestering
Phrasings Terseness
Strangles Repeaters
HORSETAIL
LITHENESS En-
grosses Hailstone
Aptly Assessing Au-
thority Tipsiness
Harassing Vagrant
Lightness Loitering
Freeways Rearrange
Alternate Thera-
bles Airliners Pol-
ish & Aerations of
and which shall not
yet be named or.
AMERICA
GOODBYE!
&goodbye Starli yuppy
Dogma passive Pol-
ishers or publishers
of less than greater
EarthlinessOur eerie
Panelist Obsessions
inter-loping Analo-
giesPharisees Saint-
lier Pre-Occupations
have been known
or inward fighting
Tigresses Relish-
ing Sorting Undu-
lated Cheekiness
Loathing Rational Shirt-

Our Nested

OH! MYLOVELY
ORPHANED SAIL
OR GOODBYE
OH MY OWN
SLEEPLESS
NIGHTS

harbinger lithewind, we
dross, histrionic, unrepentant still

Hersonnisus
at Midday

Shortly after the wreck & still some time before lunch.
Hersonnisus checked herself. Her cheeks a red flush.
She read herself briefly.

She would go for a walk.

Yes.

And so ambled down the cliffs
against pretext.

Briars catching and thatching her skirt.

                           The path a bit unstable.

Back down the way she had earlier purveyed.

                                        Returned to.

From the view,
                              remainders driven,

        she must venture out.

Her/self-explorer, herself so riven forward like an automat,
diving and driving out.

Froward as much as forward—a thus quickened pace.

Self-important—again.

Nothing hedged untoward.

As the wreck, as it were, is surely not a disaster. Is Sunday, at its very best. Sunday, names of names of hesitancy held on branches switch—what word was spoken which she had certainly now revealed to be true—or was it false? So-named, everyday named the other, fallen, scooped back up. Repeat. Eurydice—*Her, Herso*nnisus. *Herso*nnisus at Midday, again. Herso at mid-career. Amid something else. A retracing, a re-entrancement, en-traced. The steps previously taken to and from—fro and to the wreck, a first thought or was it only ever a rethinking? Beautiful in its grandeur, awful in its form.

Lunch had been brief.

Toast and tea things still scattered about, as always, scattered in a pattern only she could recognize.

Of a past present, a past particle only she might have grasped as somewhat, and of course insignificantly, with import, matter.

Hersonnisus' study, Hersonnisus' mess.

Her inability to sit still any longer. But happily so?

Her.

Apart from the constant strain in her neck—what work
must get done, work which could easily distract, occupy her
fingers, clear her mind. If only for a moment or perhaps many
built upon the next, which one foretold she would leave, she
was not sure.

She must investigate. And midday it already was. Damn.

Midday.

Midyear. Mid any being or flight she might have ever
aspired to.

She was only ever her own hero.

Her problem was in the realization of such.

And she may have only ever previously aspired to days neatly tucked and folded in at the seams, among rest. A restless and scattered hopeful— controlled order amongst disorder.

What moment was it that she had first fully encompassed herself? She couldn't presently decipher, but here she was again heading down the cliff after an uneventful lunch. Or so it would seem.

The sifts and

tulle

toward,

turning back to the self-investigation of

truth, selfhood, or lapsing *frow*ard beauty.

at the least its prescient possibility. Or, only to realize it
was biased and sophomoric cognitive faultiness. Somehow,
though, always here once again. Hersonnisus at Midday,
perhaps mid-thinking. Hersonnisus—a somanied her,
herher always erratic.

His moustache annoyed her more today than usual.

His constant hand gesturing, petting and grooming, his constant self-referenced pointing. What was that?

Really, in greater context this too may have a sign.

A sign she surely had to read and interpret.

Toward the wreck, *her* wreck and the ominous
and impending what doom.

Wreck of she's,

thus departed.

She too had faults— manied

and multiplicitous of course — but those were such an imbedded, controlled interior mess, so natural as a person's hair color or sex, that her problems would never seem small, hairy and dense all at once, should be a given of course, as why should those prepackaged issues even count at present? Her own recognition of her faults would seamingly pardon her.

That was *Her*! She, her Hersonnisus, his *Her*, as if that ever counted.

Her her her. Clutter amongst clutter. Starhewn dreamdust. So much piled and saved, or to be saved — causing its own form of distraction. Mid-flight, she looked out to the sea. Its astonishment held her. The day was clear. Finally. An interruption of so many gray and dreary. Nilled nulled mists in its net, arrested. Evolving. Seasonal. *Her her her. Repeat.* Changing.

The shoreline seemed to vary unbelievably today.

Strange minutia, entangling what mutability, perseverance at
all odds. Sea-lined faces.

Or, the sea.
                    The sea there.

                    Seathus,-
          no longer indifferent, or
              differentiating.

The sea *had* had her first, before she knew enough to stop it.
Or say no, even, as if that might have even mattered.

Faces etched, sketched and hewn among faces underlying
words. Sea bent faces, an endless seaming conquest to be
taken, or had, retaken. This half-consumed her.

As Sea, her wayward deity — her life. What had initially
saved her, could also destroy her.

Saved her but perhaps but not from the hell of those attempts
on the part of the others. It was all exhausting to think of,
her head weary and in need of repose. Slightly slanted,
its form toward the ground, a little, as she petitioned the
moment, to ground her. Pieced and resident as each glass
of Grandmother's dream-catching sunlight in soft whites
and greens— long accumulating, haring the beach picked
specifically less now.

She wandered and wandered down, finally to the shore's
edge. Clutched a piece of Seaglass. In her grip. Held it up
at arm's length, allowed it to cover the sun, held out so, as it
were. Covering all and midday. She brought the stone round
in a circle,

she paced away from the sea then.

Forward then,

She turned the stone over again in her pocket. The shoreline.
She thought:

> *Keep a stone in your pocket seven year;*
> *turn it, and keep it seven year longer,*
> *that it be ever ready to thine hand*
> *when thine enemy draws near.*

She said it again aloud. Where is that from? Surely *she* didn't
make that up?

as the cliff she had just descended, the view of the house, and
orchard, and there she could see him also pacing
to and fro.

There, among the trees. Restless. She watched him for a moment, for what seemed an eternity. Held him fast in her small stare.

Held him in his very waywardness ever opposition.

Her fault.

This was.

Seeing him human, thus fraught. Infantile.

This might obfuscate any and all way out.
Just now. Imagining He as real, he as despicable.
Human. He as a baby on his mother's chest.

Her hands then clutched her breasts,
Her Seaglass fell to her feet.
With a quick sweep, the shoreline, the sea, took it back.

At first she frantically tried to get the glass piece, half her
skirt was soaked before she gave up. Another sign?

Wild Seanotes.

Heart pounding, screeching there like a wild and
lost wet bird.

Overwhelming rested halfnotes.

Sea*sonnet*ed!
This wouldn't bring her back to him or vice versa, but this
normally would always halt her descent from *here* herein.

Seeing as need, as real, seeing past her own desire,
her own will even.

Seeing past her own fucking mess in the kitchen.

But still,

watching him now, she wondered,-

How she could ever want him in that way? Looking for a moment longer, he seemed to take pause in the field, from the relentless to and fro, from his constant step. Creeping forwards and backwards, backwards and forwards — running his hand through his hair.

Was this a gesture of disbelief, an obvious sign of weakness, of his own secluded wildness?

Moments like this occurred frequently, perception of which could be dangerous. At one time mother-held, as most were, transfixed.

The open road, giving,
nursing every need and want of
the babe at her chest, not starving notions.
Albeit his.

At her breast, rapturous heart, each desire or hope only
further encouraged. But these thoughts of his babyhood must
and will be tamped down. Imperative in her journey as it
were to getting through the wreck just after tea.

                    She must get through this wreck alive or whole.
                              But would it happen for *Her*?

She now was determined to sit where she had so long stood.
She will not allow his visage to continue to disturb her, as she
sat at her feet, the shore, and ocean waved her inward.

Perhaps the wreck a dream, perhaps the wreck gone. Inline.
What might have you. The seemingly recent, burned out
frame stood among the dunes, wild with sea-grass.

Perhaps only sun-weathered. Framing her.

The sun hit her cheeks as if the day had pardoned it.
It gave her a chill. A rash, fresh feeling. Restoration.

The new form being salt. Ressurrection.

Which she had not thought or felt, ever, until this moment. She would keep it. Go as she must or drown the ever-gasping seathus, the moment held her. Hersonnisus breathed again. And it was a new seeing then. New life in the instant.

Her. Tomorrow. Before. Her.
Her tomorrow.

Hersonnisus at midday.

SCRAWL

Or;- (from the markings of)
the small her(o)

PROEM

&

*from   Aster
Asterias*

A S T ER ASTERIAS

A REALISM LOST HER   NAME : M A R I E   (O) SHE
        SHE   STROLLS

IN HRS   NAMES MARI / S/HE   TELLS HER/E&
        HERS &HER HRS

SO(U)LS AS ASTER HARMS IRES   TELLS (O) A HARM
        IRES LETS LOS   (O)

A SEASHELL   TRIM O R,- A LARAMIE SUN- LESS
        ATLAS SIR,-

AN HRS ASTRAL ASTROL ASTROL   O( )R MUSES
        HER HAT HRS IN

& SO,- A GRANDAMES ERR   HER   LATERAL LOSS
        LOS S/ T I L L S

OR,- ONE GRANDMERES HER SALT LUNES IN
A SEAGRAMS REND

TRILLS   AS A TEAGRAM   SENT NILLS ALAS,-
LET US S U N US

SEE AT LAST UNLESS   ESTELLINA TIS SUN AS
S E A S

AS ATTIS SITS   NULL   AS SEAS TAT NETS &SO
LULL AS ALL *A A* AS U

A (S U N S/ A NS SET   AT LAST ASTIR (O) ASTER
NETS US LETS ALL*ES*

AS SE N T   US (O) AS ALL ATTENS US   ALL
ATTENS MY A T L A S T MY OUTLASTS   L(N) E TS
A L A S NESTS US

(*p r o e m*

       toward the end

of all things   surely

       lapsed

          froward

&daunting)

from the markings of the small her(o) when morning wakes
     bright

wakes unfolded new gesture in the space of or toward a
     balance or

possibility of what is and is so spoken this (o) and what
     new language spoken or

simply netted and so suited toward her as is and better is so
          suited toward   (her)

while fresh s(o) air crisp as an imperative open window like
     clockwork

airing out bed things as feathered filled dreamt things& stale
     night air

bitte   *bitte*   *bitte eh*   *eh*   *eh*   with fine repeat repeated
&again

as to turn into this world   as in flesh   &in so coming to be
born—gauntlet of

smallness   she   and her said fitting the grandest   entry she   (
o)   we   all might

ever know to only so soon forget and rely on others to impart
or translate here:

she b a l l r o o m (e d)   and she t/his (her) glove(d) outgrown
her(o)

in size and strangely dependent on what those o t h e r   eyes
w i t n e s s

in so fortunate in seeing this birded hour was and what had
    and what might

have unfolded such an entry—immer so—which is first is first
    (o) &always formed

as form must dictate surely even here then is first and perhaps
    only signified by

a dated time or occurrence— steel hands their metal chill—
    say eradication say

waving any other/or let's just say a rather brutal alternative—
    say incision

from the whole   what must signify beginning then   so began
    is ever first *is* first

is first for this o n e hero as warmth and blind light
    evacuation

from the fitted glove-like fisted quarter—unimaginable as so
    b u t

this, the first known—cramped but fitting then—breath—
    t h e n

what seems endless handling what and all that pinafore
    petticoat

pet petting as pet touch this snug chill warm attachment—as
    perfect

q u a r t e r e d compartment— god-like in its anti-quietudian
    state—t h i s

many marked beginning—cuckcooing as more feeling than
    words c o u l d

&so denote—pushed so &pushed so this vision in the beginning
    of: b e i n g

extant—what felt—what is long kept or feated—feeted so fed&
    g i v e n

step stridently so—metered smallness by extent of which is
    e n o r m o u s—

d a n c e— a walled patting nudge& swayed hiccupped
    r e l e v a n c e—

h e r(o),- as such is deemed her s m a l l l a u g h t e r surely
    s u r r o u n d i n g

: h e r (o) :

&

< < an interjection >>

t h e   s m a l l   her(o)

previously &so,- not noted
or side-noted or   all too simply
abandoned   dismissed seamingly
squashed and quelled along the side-
lines as too damn precious   or unnaturally
prescient &so crushed sentimental as such

yes, the small her(o) must surely
wonder where feeling went
toward the end of the 20th
                    century ?
when narrative and confession
begged prosaic & so chill
&so   to be
heard again   when the next
g e n e r a t i o n

m i g h t very well r e a d
this we/us
       —as dull
as is merely broken parted&
distorted us/we as thoughtless
or unduly heralded&
such &so side-stepped
in way of marginalia

     a s s o
u n f e e l i n g of the smallest
and of we this she
     our surely most unheard
s t i f l e d h e r (o)

MINARETS

ASTER   ASTIR   TATS   A   NAME   SIR,-   A   MANE
    STIR, A MEAN

S T A R A S ARE MAIN,- SIR AREMAN   ITS   NAMER
    REMAINS   ITS A N *M E*

SIT(OR   SAT)   A   NAMERS   NAME   IT   REMAINS
    TRI TRIM&TAME

M E A N T SIR,- O   A MARE SIN SIR A MARE RIN
    TINTINS A MARE

ISNT A M A R E LESS LOINS SIR AS SO SAT
    ATTIS &SO

ALESS   MAREN   INALOY   SMEARS   RIM   UNA
    REAR LIT *A S T* R E A M S

SISTERN   SE(S)T(INA)S   IN   A   MASTER   MIN
    ASTREAM *A*

A   TRAÜM   IN   O   MERE   AMATTER/S   AT
    LO I N S

A   MATE/   (T)R   SIR,-   O'HERSON   ATAMER   INS   A
    TRAINERS SIN O

SLATTERN   L A T T I S   MIT LANTERN NEAR MIST
    AS SNARE MIT

A/STA(E)R/N *A   S   T   E   R* (I) AMIT   ASTER/N/IA
    IN A MIT /

MIT   SANE   ASTROL   TRIM IN A M A T E& S O RISEN
    TATS A SEER OR

NEAT   STAR   AT   SEA-TIME   UNSERE/
    O( )R DEAR MINARETS

AM(A)RISEN   SET   A   MARIS   NET   NESTS
    AN ASTERN SET

NET   I   M   N   AS   AN   MIT   MIT   STAR-RENTS
    AN MARIA ASSENTS

SENT ASTIR &NESTED   HER   SEALESS   HRS   URN
    NEST-TURNS

LETS LUNA LOS (LASSEN) A TERSE RIME ASSA S E N T
    (I) RAN MIT

INA ALAS MET ATTEM &RAINED STEMS   &SO I
    R A N LOS

&SO RAN MET   A SIREN MET ASTERIA   AMIDST
    HER SIREN TRAIN

UNS AMISS A   S T E R N / E N (*) MET ANON
    A SAINT   HER

SATIN STRAND MER-A -MATE   O A SIREN S E T :
    A R T E M I S   TATS

HER N A M E A S T I R   ASTER   ASTERIA
    O SIR,- UNSERE

MANE STIR, A M E A N *S T A R / A S* A SISTER AS A SET
    UNSERE DEAR MINARETS,

UNSERE SANE SISTER INSEL SETS TIS SATE(D)
    ASTER ASTERIA

and all this when her coming &all is so needfull and
  inevitably so

as it always was so oddly demanding and seductive in its
  speechless revelatory stasis

provoked   as   any   suns   previous   "I"   might   as
  those whom set eyes

upon her and had wondered or imagined when s/he &
  this her(o) her

prescience   desirable as any   as small she &overlooked
  she (in way of voice) —

wayward sheward wary she so pointed always gives new
  breath as she is   so surly bent

Hyper-Phantasie
Constructs

'Ich bin so Vielfach!'

'Wie bunt entfaltet sich mein Anderssein...'

Emmy Hennings

(one)

InvestedPrayerSieTenderlein

\>>So Vielfach!<< I am
I   am I
Populaire!

Bookwood traumen, always
of pine green forest
I, of hem-lined Seas
I, of Ifs and possibility
dillettante derelectic
so many   so multiplicitous
So manied movingward eras
errored &enamoring lovely
multiplicities

(one)

Hyper-Phantasie Constructs

HomeSayings: Friendship with
Concepts of — Contrame Tobacco born In
DUexcerpts affaires from
HAcking Culture InWardness
BlastBlastBlast elemental
Weak Cloaks All Rooted
Literary HollowHeads
To Be Against is to BE—
Politico Progressive
ALLFED Pretended Aversion
WAT IS...Cities of Light &Gardens
Unemployment Tretet Certainty Truth&
Life Experience Taken with Dirty Linen Spoonings
Serious Meaning Worths Trembleless
Plaster Scandal Relief in Clouded monies
InvestedPrayerSieTenderlein

(one)

mundane false strides
process corporate overload
process alt societies during
hyper-fantasy constructs

what strange beings

daily riding swanky beat
in tandem navigating
mundane false strides

(one)

fabric in &of itself

pamphlets forming
pages& so on of ink

Slatted curious
what strange beings

(one)

SeaProw meaning obsolete —

In the sense of profit
Paper, Creation in the &new
kinds of versions &endless
geographies &thus the very
fabric in&of itself

(one)

Ventures Prowesse

Estrin Vigors
tales of Valor
prouesse, from proece (Fr. prouesse),
from prou, of prud
SeaProw meaning obsolete —

(one)

Squatted Mew

Masculine-Age Portraiture

dehumanization

erasure of —

SELF

valorized embrace

(one)

A Filched Turmoil Sown
Ours

Ultimo Sun Sorrows
Mien Rumours Wost

Stowed pitchfork
Searching for
Subterranean vestiges
paperworked talents

Squatted
Mew

(one)

Melting, We wake.

Drowning out our Night Ships.

We wake.

Appearing to reinvent propriety.

We wake.

Pretending we are not

We wake.

Are we not really just curious animals at the end of
the day?

We wake.

Apparently renewed and whole and pure.

We wake.

Forward, Undaunted.

We wake.

Undressing each step before us.

We wake.

Inconsistent, Irreverent, Contradicting.

(one)

All packed-In
Refuting,-
The female as an index
Or,- "He" becoming the alluring one as "she"
Subjects transgressing pigeonholes—US garnered
gender machines
Or, as Portrait,

She—
fisti-cuffed, little slip of a thing
He against—her (yet
Untested, Relentless Love-Inspiring Machine)

Caught pulsating, white heated arrows
in the hum&turn of Night
Melting

(one)

Negating Negation
Social Uraniums
as Malicious Runs
My Calumnious Sir

An Aqua Figure So,-
In Rued Fog I go

Augers Saga Of Is
Quasi Urges Or,-
A Foe Rug, A Roues Fig

Rousing Figures Thus

Ego Für I
Fir Uns In
Goer Inns Us
Aquae IF Forged
from Ruins

Rogued Ifs:
A Sea. A Sofa. A Quay.
The Unbound Sea.

(one)

Death As constant ambulation

Aдo Aдo Aдo!
Consistent fetch and retrieval
negotiation where one shouldn't be

Negating Negation

(one)

faineantise me, she sighed...

Fadaise or,-
Idea as
Aide as idea not
a side

Sea If
Safe
Safe I As
Feen Fade As I
Deaf As I
Fade-Sea I As
Sea-Fade I As
Death As

(one)

Doth animate, reanimate
digitalized fife uprising

faineantise me, she sighed.

(one)

weariful cast-iron hoodlums

Our turmoils in filched onus rows
worsted muslin throws, we

all remain We
keep our book of days
Unwritten

Symbolic — Outworn
steeped meanings
sewn luminous

each gesture a new lexicon

freewheels reinvent mirth too
Restive thorn mints Veriest
Inverse Riveters
Doth,-

(one)

The Unbound Sea

Her Smooth Box Full

and so, ergo she

to poetry

      what insistent fortuitous

way-side collisions   [extraordinaire!]

harmless smatterings   miraculous
feminine decorativeness

marking her posterity

      and so, ergo she, again

inexplicable
             everturning

Susana Gardner's first full-length collection of poems, *[lapsed insel weary]* was published by The Tangent Press in 2008. She has published several chapbooks, including *Hyper-Phantasie Constructs* (Dusie Kollektiv, 2010) and *Herso* (University of Theory and Memorabilia Press, 2009). Her poetry has appeared in many online and print publications including Jacket Magazine, How2, Puerto Del Sol, and Cambridge Literary Review among others. Her work has also been featured in several anthologies, including "131.839 slog meth bilum" (131.839 keystrokes with spaces), NTAMO, Finland and NOT FOR MOTHERS ONLY, a collection of poetry by women from Fence Books, USA. She lives in Zürich, Switzerland, where she also edits and curates the online poetics journal and experimental kollektiv press, Dusie, www.dusie.org.